WALLABY

THE OFFICIAL ART OF
2010

Text compiled and captioned by Jonathan A. Zimbert
Sketches by Syd Mead
Still photos by Bruce McBroom and Virgil Mirano
Storyboards by George Jensen

A WALLABY BOOK
Published by Pocket Books
NEW YORK

Another *Original* publication of Wallaby Books

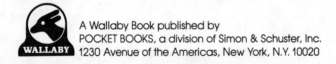

A Wallaby Book published by
POCKET BOOKS, a division of Simon & Schuster, Inc.
1230 Avenue of the Americas, New York, N.Y. 10020

ISBN: 0-671-54336-9

First Wallaby Books printing December, 1984

10 9 8 7 6 5 4 3 2 1

WALLABY and colophon are registered trademarks
of Simon & Schuster, Inc.

Printed in the U.S.A.

Peter's wonderful Vision,
Frank—the greatest Leo ever,
Elliot's "whatever needs to be done, will be,"
and Judy—for her eternal support.

INTRODUCTION

The professional challenge of contributing to a motion picture with the dimensions of *2010* is always exhilarating. The imagination races ahead with premature ideas and images; creative design schedules are checked for possible conflicts in available time, and a first meeting with the director is anticipated.

On Friday, May 27, 1983, Richard Edlund, SFX director for the *Star Wars* Trilogy, called me to find out if I would be interested in working on a movie. Naturally! The first meeting with Peter Hyams, the director of *2010*, was in a charming gourmet restaurant on Santa Monica Boulevard simply to meet.

Avoiding the unproductive waste of time is one of the reasons my design projects cover so many subject areas. Coming up with new ideas can be made an efficient process if two important conditions are satisfied. The first is accurate information about the job; the second is finding out what makes a particular job unique. These criteria were satisfied by the fact that Peter Hyams was writing the screenplay in satellite communication with Arthur C. Clarke, author of *2010 (The Odyssey Continues)* and was intimately involved in establishing the dramatic end-use of the various designs generated for the feature.

A meeting was scheduled for June 2 at Peter's MGM office. From the general conversation at our get-acquainted breakfast, I knew that the design for the *Leonov* was first priority. Not only was it important "how" it should look, but "why" it should look that way. That first meeting clarified overall proportion and assembly rationale for this very utilitarian spaceship. We were 85% there on the "look" of the *Leonov*.

An education in industrial design benefited me with a sensitivity to the intricate process ideas must go through to become "real" things. A simplification of this process can be stated as a three-phased progression: idea, documentation, and production. Certainly the process is highly interdependent, but without the initial idea, nothing gets produced. There are many more people trained to "make" things than there are to "think" things. This fortunate imbalance keeps me busy on many different kinds of projects.

With accurate information as to what the end result is to be, one can carefully synthesize the whole process mentally, and produce sketches or photographically accurate renderings of the finished "thing." Is this design? Absolutely. In the specific case of working with the film industry on future features, this process is a very exotic mixture of technical speculation and appreciation of the audience's capacity for recognizing and accepting something as a believable, dramatic prop. This is much different, incidentally, from creating things for industry.

The *Leonov* was envisioned by Peter Hyams as a working environment in space, with rockets attached for propulsion. Very sober, very Russian, and considerably over-engineered; a purposeful machine to get a crew to Jupiter and observe the strange phenomena occurring there. My job was to assist the director's interpretation of the story with hardware that would look appropriate and technologically believable. At first, I drew the forward control stem as a projection at 10 degrees off the ship's main axis, on the premise that not only did it look interestingly awkward, but also allowed sight lines past the rotating crew block. Peter preferred, however, to keep the ship on one axis. We proceeded this way, and started adding detail keyed to the various function sections of the ship.

The "look" of something is subtlely enhanced by keeping a consistency in the detail; perhaps all edges have a certain section, or detail occurs only around the edges of panels. If the same type of detail is maintained, the "thing" will have continuity and a logic all to itself no matter how fanciful. This continuity is what I kept reinforcing while working on the various sections and mechanical additions to the *Leonov*.

What kinds of concessions does one make when dealing with the visualization of future technology? Originally, I had proposed a four-stage, unfolding ion propulsion system, assuming that nine years after the *Discovery*, this kind of drive would be available . . . a huge, glowing, blue umbrella at the rear of this somewhat ungainly craft. In order to accommodate a climactic scene near the end of the story, Peter needed an impressive display of power, an explosive ignition of engines to dramatize the moment. Answer? Two main rockets, four secondary rockets, and six vernier rockets in side-mounted swivel housings—twelve in all! Much more dramatic than the silent glow of ion drive.

This illustrates the difference between corporate and motion-picture design clientele. A corporation decides to change the way a product works or create an entirely new kind of product for the consumer. Millions of dollars are spent to design it, the buying public is educated to recognize this marvelous new thing, and more than likely, taught a new word for it. A lexicon of function terms may be needed, as well.

A motion picture is an illustrated story. The illustration is a supportive part of the whole, and the "in head" memory of the audience must be used in order to make the combination work. If the prop or setting seems inappropriate, the story's world is damaged. My creations are characterizations specifically designed to make the story's world believable. They must look like they have been designed, manufactured, and put into use by the inhabitants of the story.

As a designer, my illustration ability is a convenience both for myself and for my clients: for myself, because I can illustrate my ideas and control their presentation; and for my clients by showing their ideas in use with mood, people, and the accessories of an everyday life-style. No matter how photographic or dramatic, however, my limitation is that I must pick only one view at a time. The presentation is static and two-dimensional. Not so, of course, with moving pictures. The first time I visited the *Blade Runner* set, for instance, I was walking through one of my small gouache street sketches. Seeing the *2010* sets for the first time, with their detail and finish so brilliantly constructed by *2010*'s production designer, Albert Brenner, was like wandering through the sheets of my own sketch pad. Seeing the comm room, the bridge, and the cavernous EVA pod bay was a genuine reward.

The EVA pods were the most elaborate of several additional hardware items I created. The ideal direction was to produce a one-man telephone booth enclosure abundantly encrusted with mechanical add-on detail, and having an awkward and difficult-to-use look. These specific end results were accomplished in the same way that I would achieve a deliberate visual effect for a corporate client—by selectively altering detail, angular relationships, and relative proportions of the various parts of the design. The cabin was placed between three vertical legs. At first, I adhered to zero-gravity reality and showed the legs as spindly shock tubes and articulated pads. Peter pointed out the fact that with the outer-space lighting conditions, the legs would disappear in long shots. I increased the diameter of the legs and their supporting struts, and enlarged some of the exterior hardware. The finished EVA pod is an exact three-dimensional duplicate of the finished and approved second-generation sketch.

Another major hardware item was the ship-to-ship transfer system; a kind of 2010 bosun's chair. For dramatic reasons, Peter Hyams did not want an enclosed tube or a rigid fixture to connect *Discovery* and the *Leonov*. The fragility of a series of frames strung together on barely perceivable cables would produce the same apprehension as those heaving, unstable rope bridges strung across chasms in countless jungle movies. The result was a series of 60-degree triangular frames, each with its own stored nylon cable set, and a contact frame with super-cooled magnets to match the diameter of the entry port on the *Discovery*. The system was stored around the EVA personnel port on the lower mast section of the *Leonov*. To make the scheme work, the hand-manipulated thruster was another item of hardware to be designed. This resembled an oversized fire extinguisher. An astronaut would exit the EVA personnel port, unlatch the transfer frame system, proceed to stretch the series of frames and cable sets between the two crafts, center the contact frame, switch on the magnets and establish a tenuous but convenient corridor for travel between the two spacecrafts!

My particular contribution in the creation of the various hardware items for *2010* then moved inside the *Leonov*. Set design, construction, and dressing are themselves an art. My contribution was to invent the intense, claustrophobic detail look of the bridge room with the captain's station, the navigation console with its overhead video cluster, the communications bay, and the personnel sleeping cabins. Al Brenner and Peter Hyams had established the various floor plans to satisfy filming crew requirements, together with the technical needs of set utility and electronic support. Using these blueprints, I put a technologically believable arrangement of detail onto surfaces. The results are absolute alternate reality.

One fascinating concession to the submarine enclosure atmosphere that was pursued in the design of the sets was the deliberate creation of a periscope. In outer space? Why not? The salient visual components that everybody thinks of when you say "periscope" are something large that comes down out of the ceiling, a horizontal rotary element, and various instrumenta-tion. Keeping the traditional cliché intact, I added monitors, a bitpad table surface, and banks of readouts. The result, actually fabricated by Al and his staff, is spectacular!

Contemporary computer image generation competes directly with the cost of models for film use. In terms of time, however, the density of varied detail can still be done best by model builders applying accumulative bits and pieces. The *Leonov* model was built by Entertainment Effects Group under the critical guidance of Mark Stetson. This was a particularly enjoyable association for me because Mark was chief model maker on *Blade Runner.* The *Leonov* is one of the most elaborately detailed movie models ever built. Initially, usual model-building procedures were changed to favor the *Leonov*'s intricate, three-dimensional design. Mark and I discussed Peter's insistence on a see-through scale reality, and the components were built as separate elements for assem-bly, much as a real ship would be fabricated. After the countless hours of inspired invention, detail application, and final painting by the skilled crew at EEG, the result is true alternate reality. The *Leonov* model is spectacular.

As I was working with Peter Hyams on refining the cabin block details for the *Leonov* model, publicity scheduling required an announcement illustration. On a Tuesday late in July 1983, Peter and I agreed on the composition for this illustration. I followed his request to show just enough of the *Leonov* ship to intrigue, but not give away the entire look of the craft. The star child from the ending of *2001* was depicted floating in a bubble. The bubble, in this case, was the earth with the Arabian peninsula, the Mediterranean Sea, and the cradle of civilization as surface detail. All of this was superimposed on the enigmatic Monolith floating above the immense orb of Jupiter. Two Jovian satellites, Io and Europa, were depicted in fictional juxtaposition as composition elements.

The last hardware item, the Probe, was created and the proportion drawings completed in December 1983. Other projects were already in progress, includ-ing a large airframe interior, a large yacht project, and several illustration commissions. I was to be involved with *2010* again in March 1984. Peter Hyams had requested a dummy cover for a prop *OMNI* magazine. The intent was to use the same art for the real *OMNI* cover in December to coincide with the feature's release. I submitted three composition choices to Peter and the finished artwork was sent to New York on May 1.

Finally, my feelings on the experience of working on *2010.* My appreciation of the high levels of expertise required to bring this kind of production to the screen was renewed. The always rewarding experience of making new friends in this exotic industry made the project very enjoyable. And, finally, watching the elaborate creation of an alternate reality, I realized with a surreal shock that when it is all over, nothing "solid" will exist except a few mementos, discarded scraps of set detail, and a vast archive of visual impressions. The real part of it all, of course, will be the vivid memories in the minds of millions who love and appreciate this very durable genre, the science fiction story, and the craft which gives the written story the dynamic realism of motion pictures.

SYD MEAD: VISUAL FUTURIST: *2010*

PREFACE

On May 16, 1983, Peter Hyams walked onto the MGM lot in Culver City having just finished the novel *2010: Odyssey Two.* The head of the studio, Frank Yablans, asked Peter if he could deliver the film version by Christmas '84. Peter felt it could be done (barring some act of God) and he soon began working on the screenplay. Production designer Albert Brenner and visual futurist Syd Mead (*Blade Runner, Tron*) were hired two months later and, together with Peter, began creating the design of the new spacecraft *Leonov.* Richard Edlund (*Raiders of the Lost Ark, Star Wars* Triology, *Ghostbusters*) was picked to supervise the visual effects for the film. When *Leonov*'s exterior design was complete, Edlund's model-making crew started tooling up. Three months later, set construction began on stages 15 and 30 while Hyams was only halfway through the script. When a start date of February 6 was decided upon, unit manager Neil Machlis began breaking down and budgeting the picture. Hyams met with Roy Scheider, who was his first choice to play the lead role. He showed him the 75 pages he had so far, and Roy loved them. He was aboard shortly thereafter. Within three weeks, Bob Balaban and John Lithgow were also cast. Beginning in December, weekly production meetings were held with all department heads so that everyone knew what was required of them. The movie began shooting as planned on February 6 and wrapped May 24, one year and a week after Peter said yes to the scriptless project. Throughout the summer he cut the film, usually without most of the complicated opticals that Richard was busily working on. And this Christmas, at a theater near you . . .

CHAPTER I
THE *LEONOV*

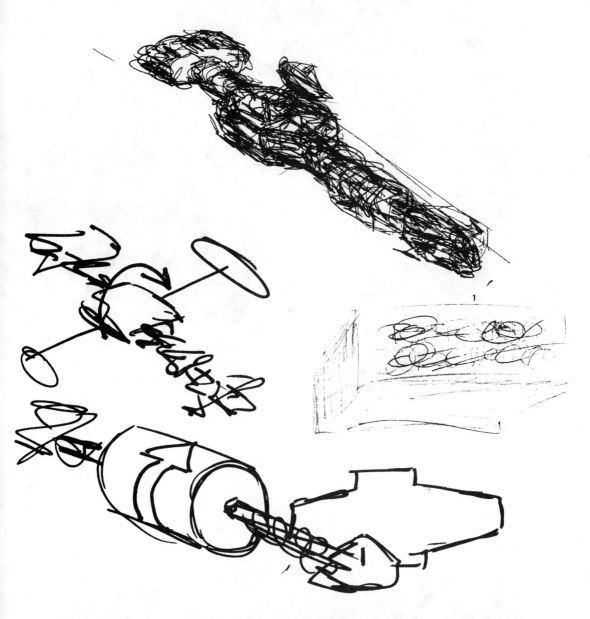

This was Hyams' first drawing of the *Leonov*, which included the idea for a spinning section to create gravity. Originally, the spinning section was created so that the movie could be filmed in a gravity condition, thereby avoiding the screen problem of twenty-minute floating/walking scenes. Then, when JPL and Boeing were brought into the act they remarked how accurate the portrayal of the ship was. The new designs for long-distance space flight include a similar rotating structure.

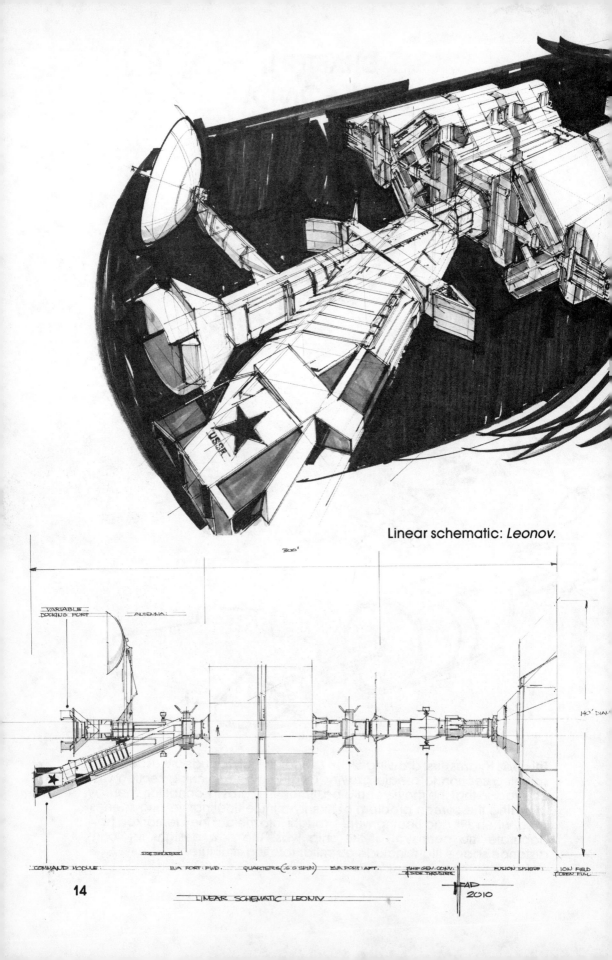

Linear schematic: *Leonov.*

300'

VARIABLE
DOCKING PORT   ANTENNA

140' DIAM

COMMAND MODULE   EVA PORT FWD.   QUARTERS (.6 G SPIN)   EVA PORT AFT.   SHIP GEN. CONV.   FUSION SPHERE   ION FIELD
                                                                                          & SIDE THRUSTERS   TOKEN FULL

LINEAR SCHEMATIC : LEONOV   2010

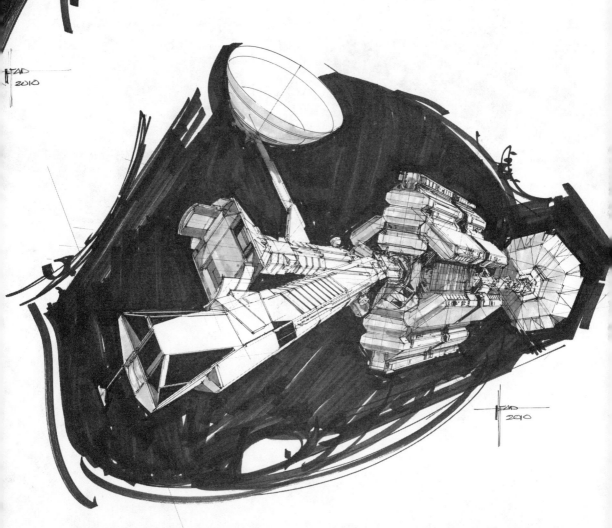

This was Syd's first pass at the *Leonov.* The long section at the bottom would have been the bridge.

Another look at Syd's first *Leonov.* Hyams had several problems with this version. Most importantly, it would make the docking sequence of *Discovery* look awkward.

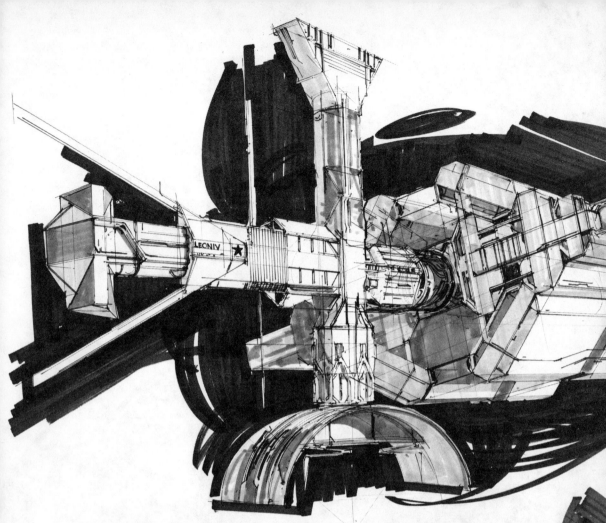

The next pass put the docking ring on the bottom and compacted the ship together. The two Prongs in front were for the heat shield.

Final version of the *Leonov*. Note the complete lack of windows except in the nose. This helped create the claustrophobic feeling of modern space travel.

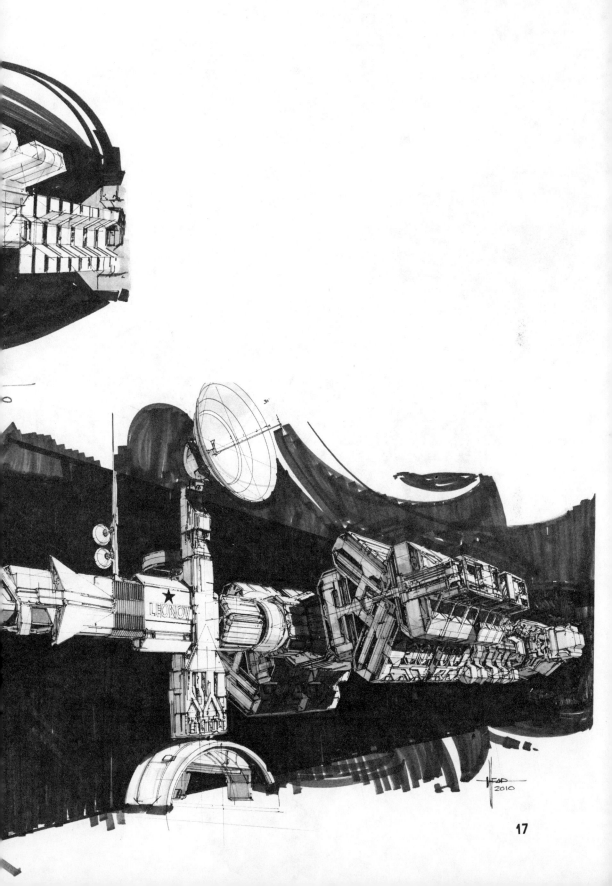

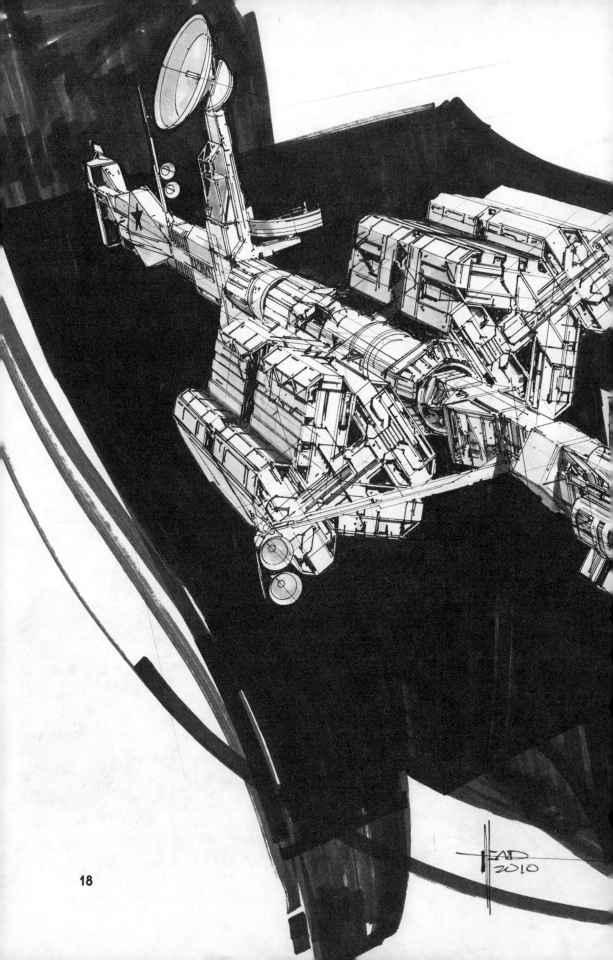

The spinning section is more apparent here. In this area, the crew quarters, medical bay, data bay, and ward/recreation room are located.

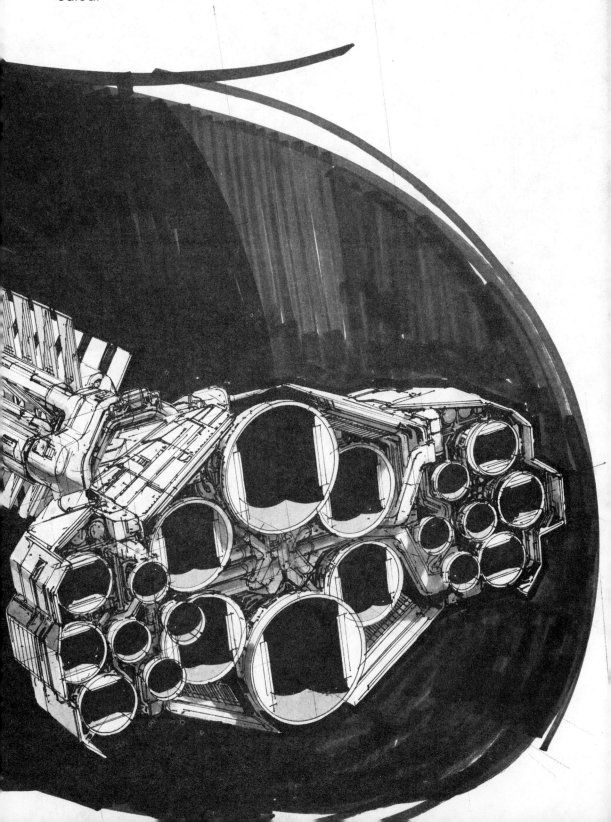

The completed model of the *Leonov.*

The Chinese ship was eliminated from the movie for two dramatic reasons. Hyams felt that space was getting too congested and that more mystery was created by not knowing what was down on Europa. In any event, here is Hyams' humorous idea of the Chinese ship.

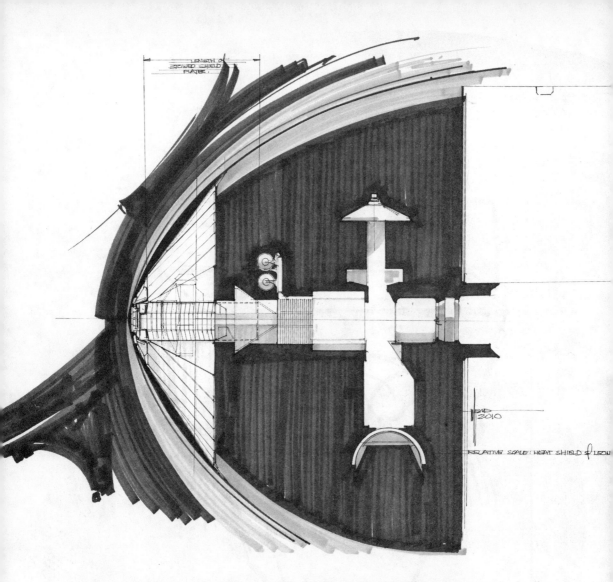

Several ideas were toyed with for the aerobraking sequence. In the novel, Clarke writes about a heat shield that is tucked away and folds out at the proper time.

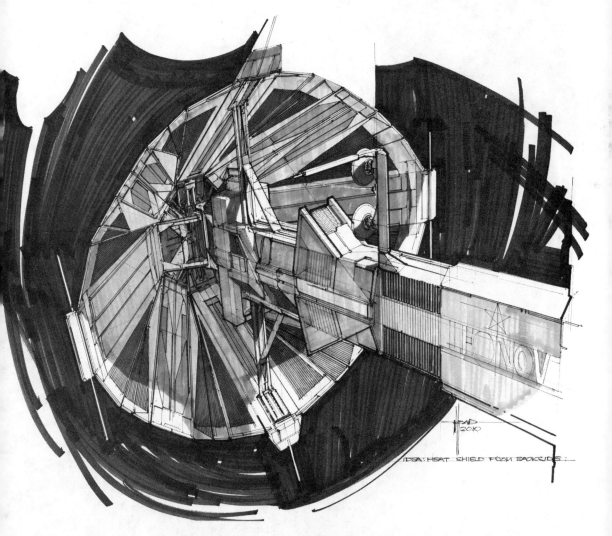

The heat shield from the backside.

This is how it would work. Note the antennae are folded down to avoid roasting.

Ultimately, after consulting with JPL and Boeing people, Hyams learned that the newest designs for aerobraking did not involve a heat shield. The shields are too weighty and take up too much room. Thus, was born the ballute—an inflatable heat-resistant shield. The ship turns aft, the ballute opens up and as the engines idle, the heat is deflected around the vessel.

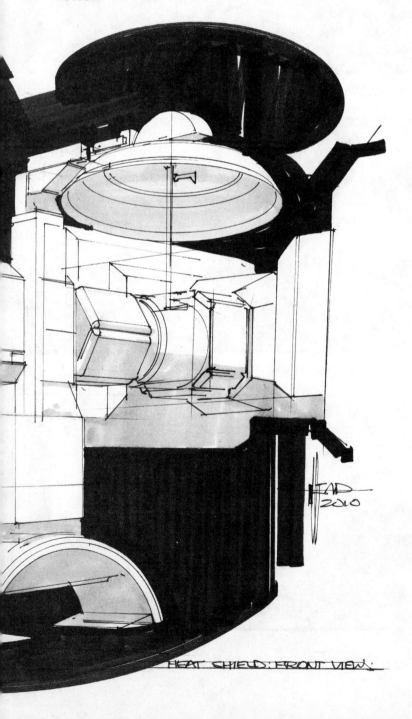

HEAT SHIELD: FRONT VIEW:

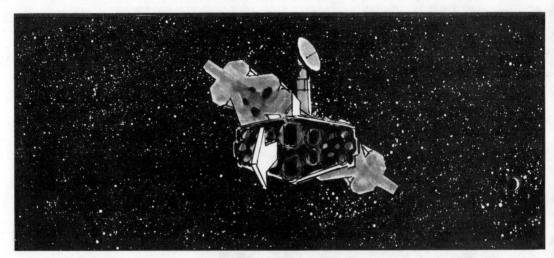

Leonov drifts backward as it prepares to deploy the ballute.

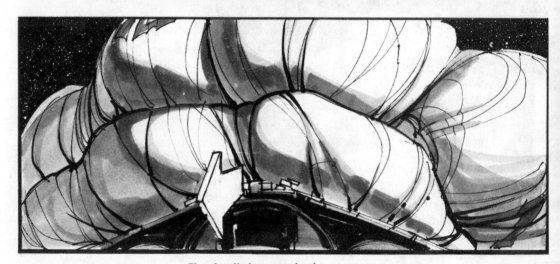

The ballutes explode open.

A section of a ballute fills the screen with orange graphics.

As the ship moves, the engines fire—shock waves and vapor trail begin to form.

Tiny, fiery shooting star travels by the ring of Jupiter.

|◄—| TRAVEL DISTANCE IN 5 SECONDS.

Tiny glow in the distance. Great contrail in foreground.

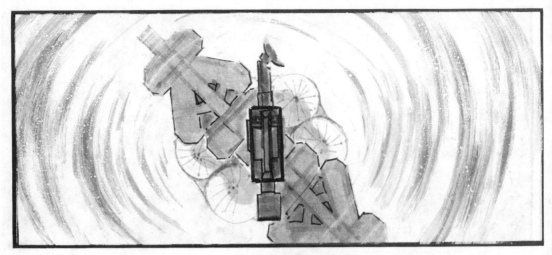

Inside the contrail, as the *Leonov* moves away from us.

LENS MOVES WITH LEONOV.

Jupiter clouds streak by beneath the *Leonov.*

Leonov streaks past lens. — LESS EFX

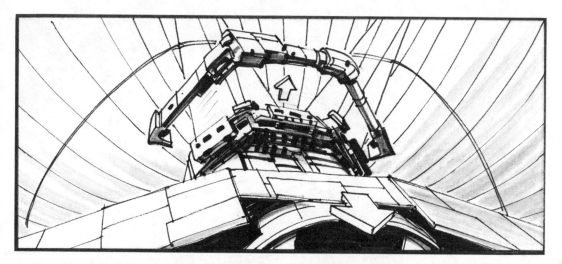

After aerobraking is complete, the ballutes are detached.

Ballutes are jettisoned from *Leonov* and float away.

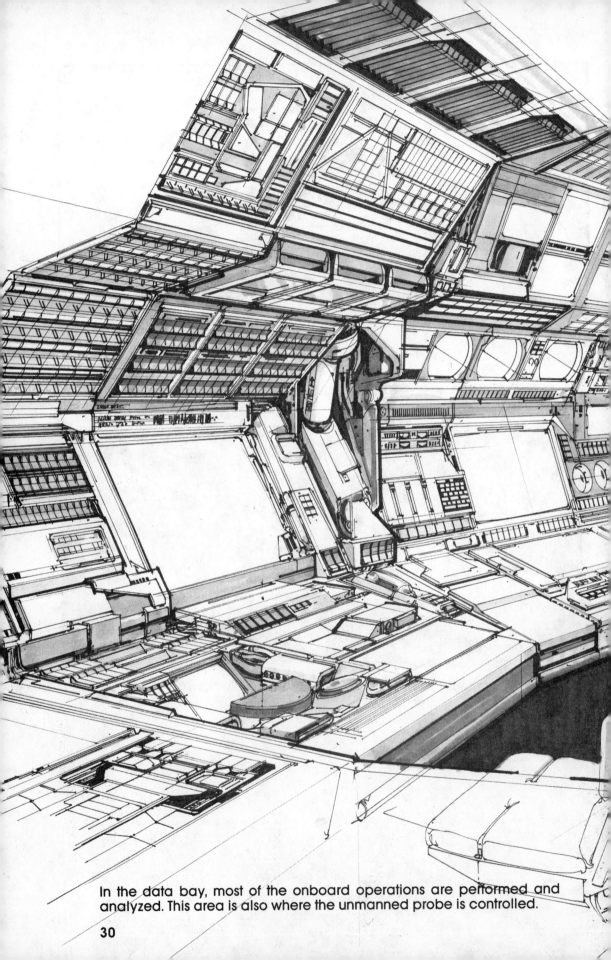

In the data bay, most of the onboard operations are performed and analyzed. This area is also where the unmanned probe is controlled.

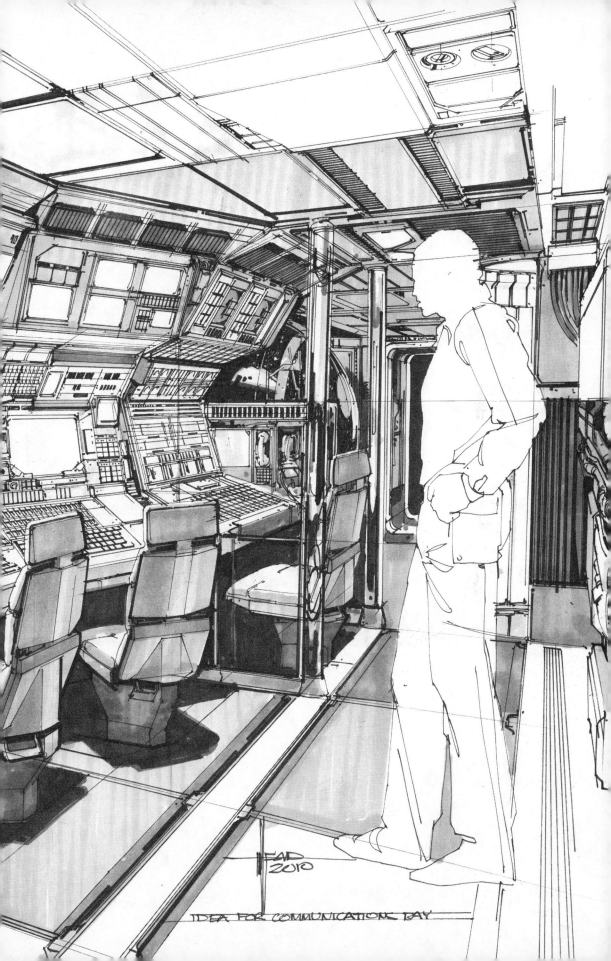

IDEA FOR COMMUNICATIONS BAY

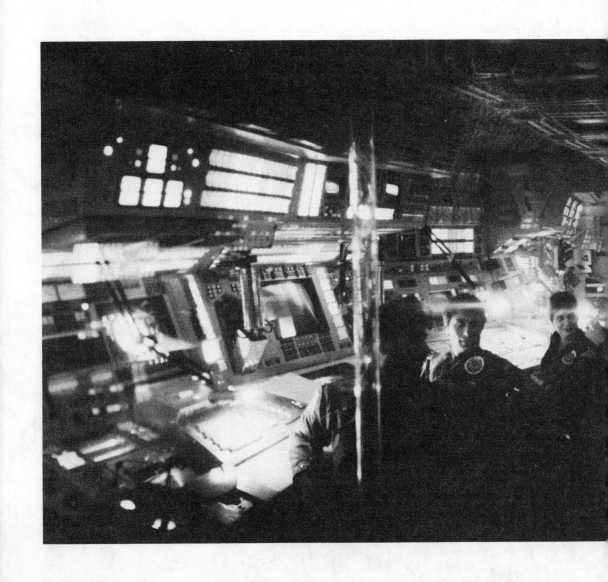

The data bay of the *Leonov.*

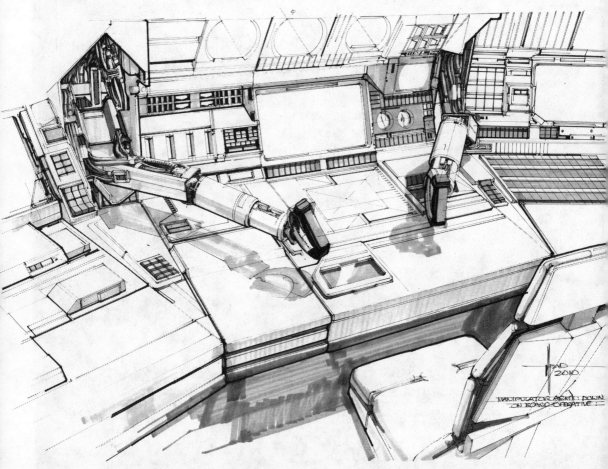

Detail of how the unmanned probe is controlled.

Reverse of prior still as Orlov and Floyd anxiously stare at monitors in search of life on Europa.

Note the live-action monitor and graphic representation/analysis of live picture. In this scene, the probe makes its way down to the surface of Europa and is ultimately destroyed.

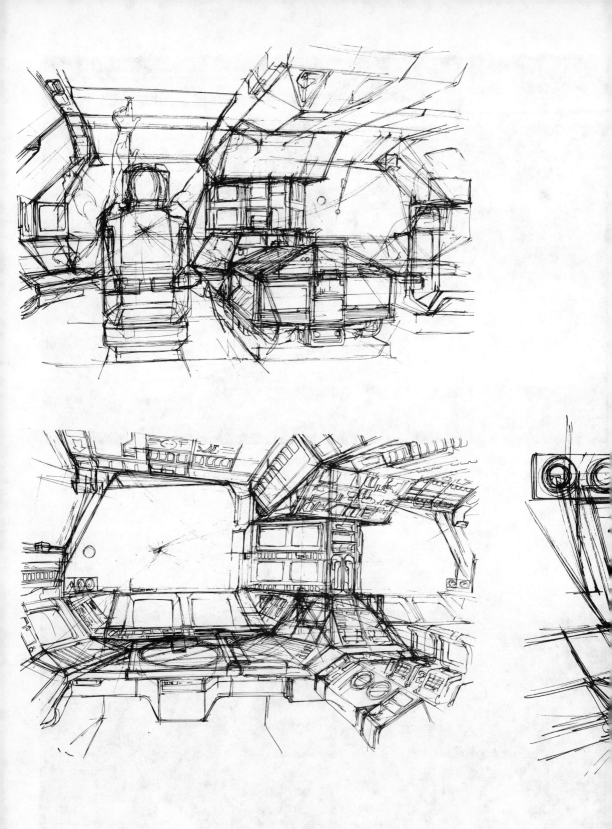

These were Syd's rough sketches for the pilots' station.

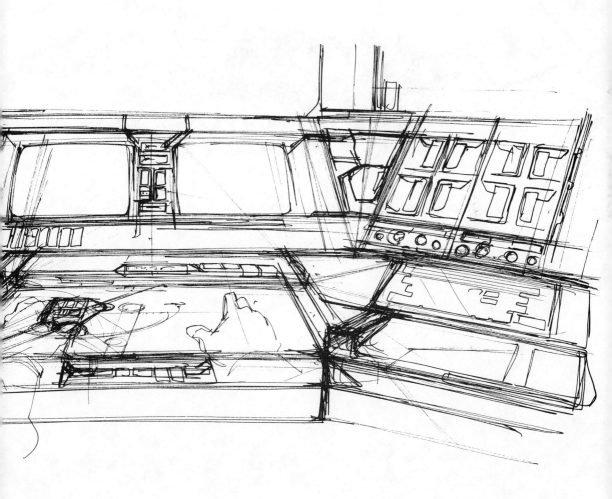

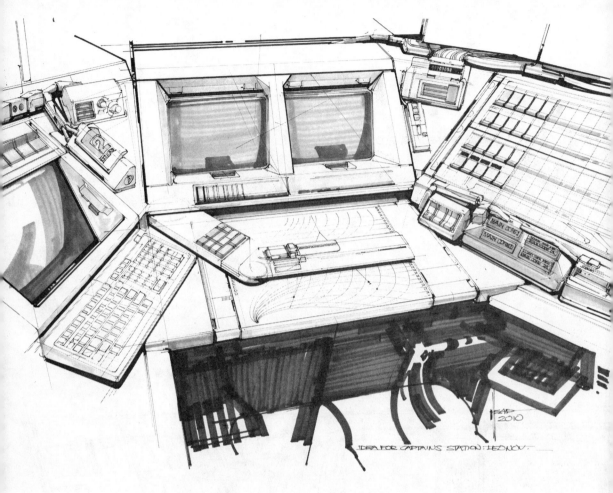

IDEA FOR CAPTAINS STATION : LEONOV.

Hyams ultimately altered it to make it look more complex.

This final cockpit design is based more on the Concorde and the Shuttle, with a futuristic twist.

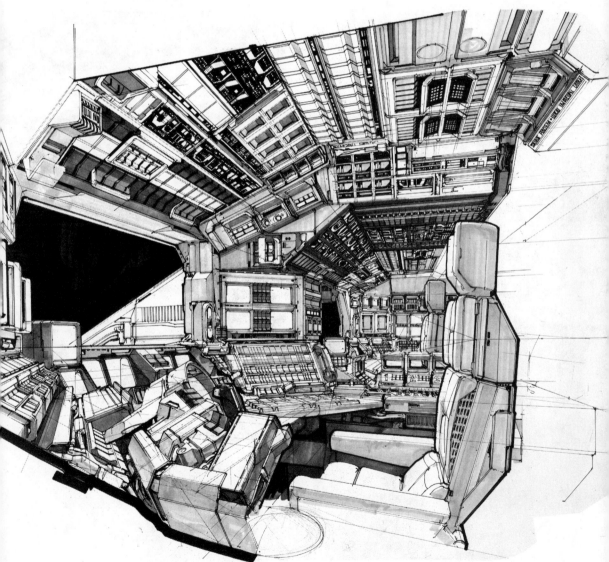

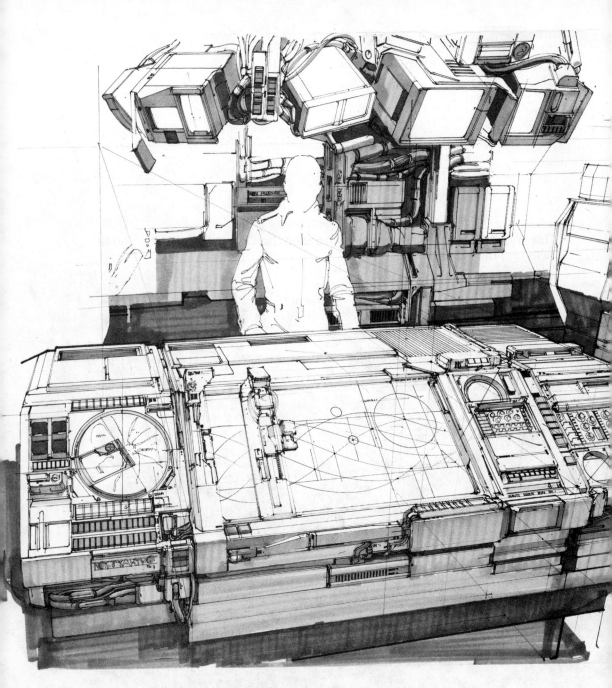

This is the navigation console located in the bridge.

The navigation console and bridge inside the *Leonov*.

Captain Kirbuk operates the *Leonov*.

IDEA FOR SURFACE DETAIL: BERTH.

This is a sleeping berth. Though it looks roomy . . .

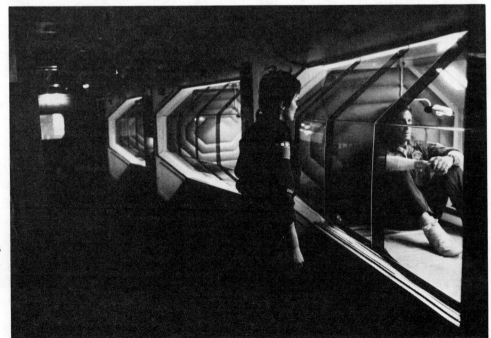

. . . it's not.

The ward room.

The rec room/lounge area.

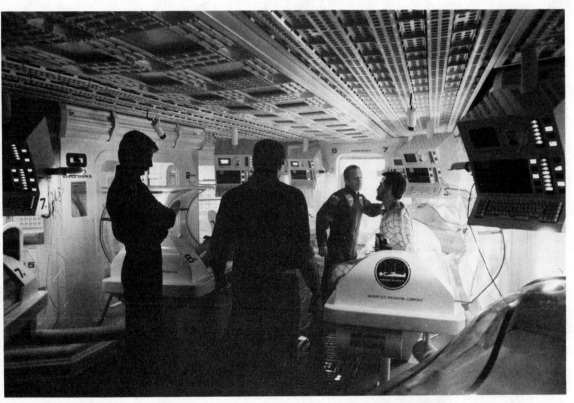

In the medical bay, some of the astronauts are put into suspended animation and monitored.

The *Leonov* pod bay.

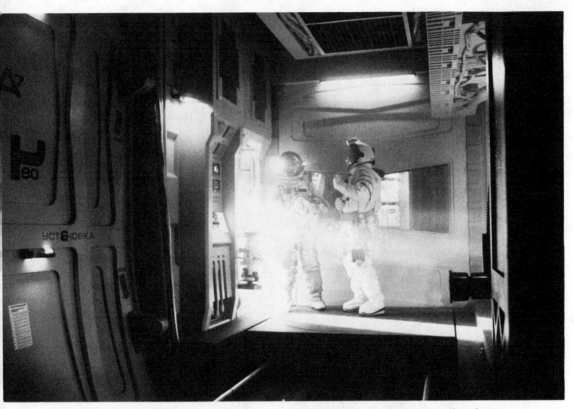

Curnow (Lithgow) and Brailovsky (Baskin) prepare to leave the *Leonov*.
Behind them is the hatchway that leads to the pod bay.

48

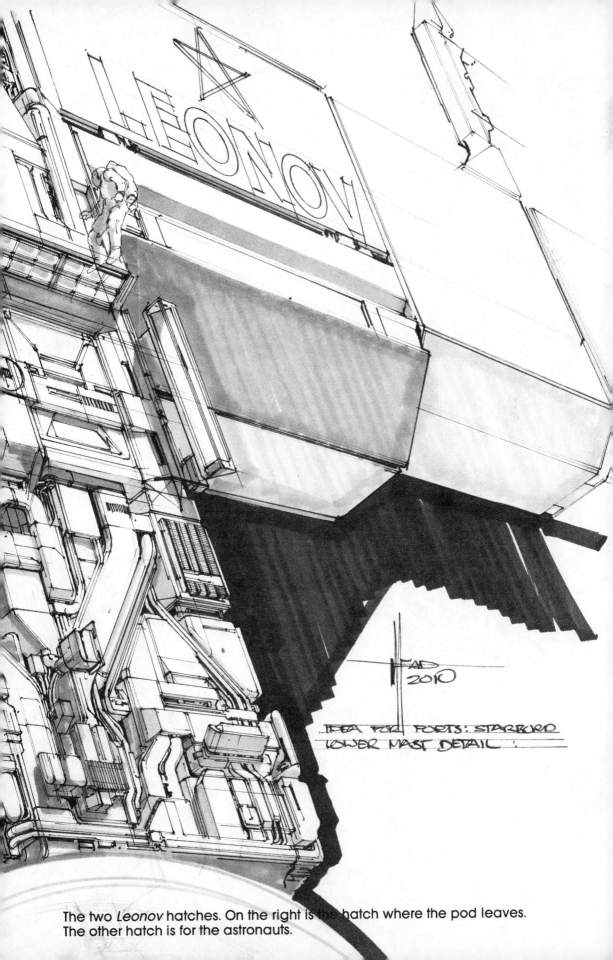

The two *Leonov* hatches. On the right is the hatch where the pod leaves.
The other hatch is for the astronauts.

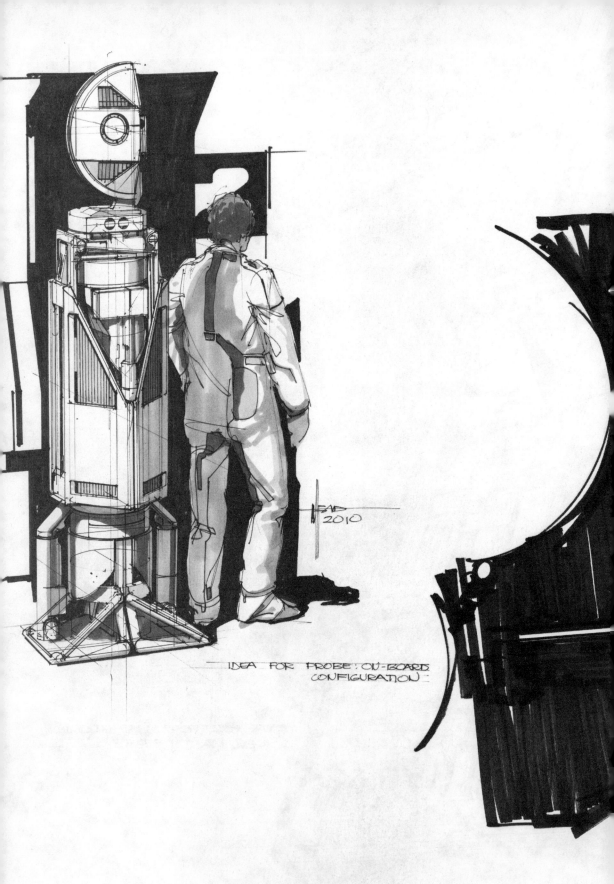

IDEA FOR PROBE : ON-BOARD
CONFIGURATION

These were some ideas for probes. Hyams wanted them a little more like Mariner and Voyager.

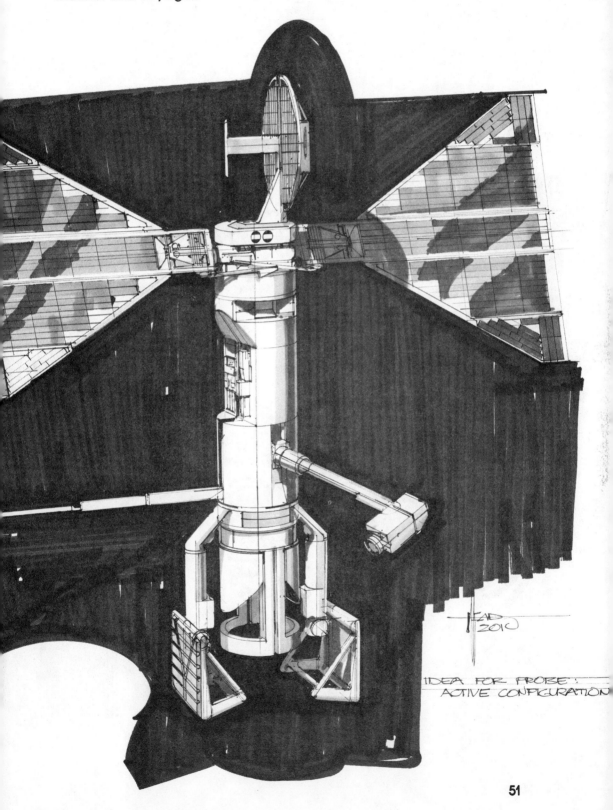

IDEA FOR PROBE:
ACTIVE CONFIGURATION

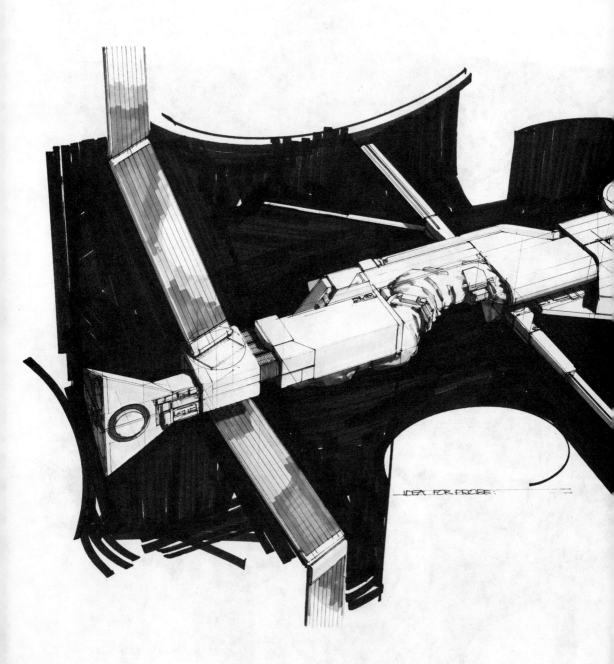

IDEA FOR PROBE.

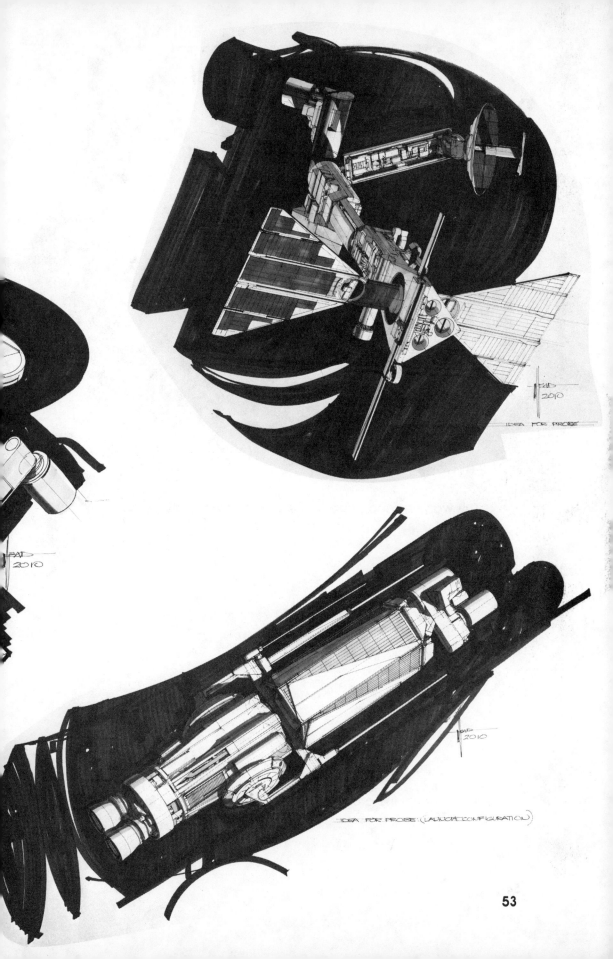

IDEA FOR PROBE

IDEA FOR PROBE (LAUNCH CONFIGURATION)

53

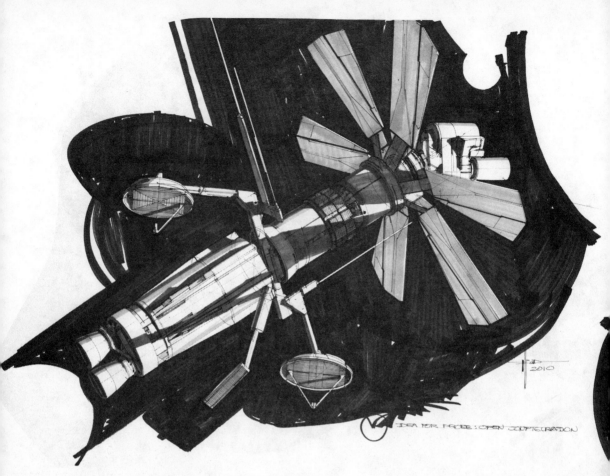

IDEA FOR PROBE : OPEN CONFIGURATION

This was the second pass at the probe, but it was still not right.

The final idea for the probe. Note that the camera is all that survived from the first passes.

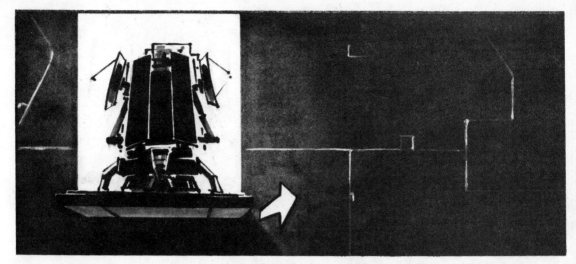

This is the sequence involving the probe and Europa. The probe begins to lift off.

Probe jets fire—it lifts off platform.

Probe clears platform and descends as the solar panels activate.

Probe deployed from starboard side of *Leonov* and climbs into the dark side of Europa.

Probe makes its way to Europa.

← ⟵ PAN TO REVEAL SUN

Tiny probe, white against black, as it descends to Europa.

Floyd's POV: We begin to see surface detail of Europa.

EXT. planet and probe.

Floyd edges in closer as probe gets lower.

The probe skims along surface.

Monitor: Moving along Europa's surface heading into the sun—the crater is seen in the distance.

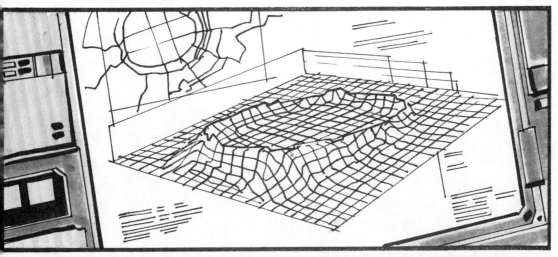

Floyd's POV: Another monitor displaying analysis of crater—something is down there.

Spotlight searches in the darkness for signs of life.

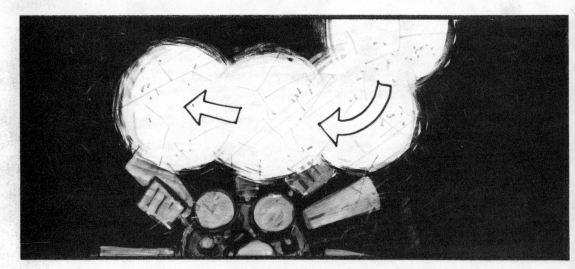

The spotlight continues to search.

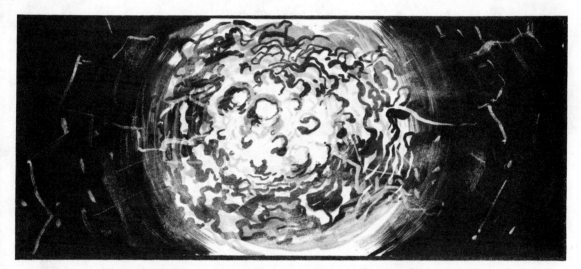

The light finds the mass as we begin to focus in . . .

. . . the monitor screen flares white, the probe is destroyed.

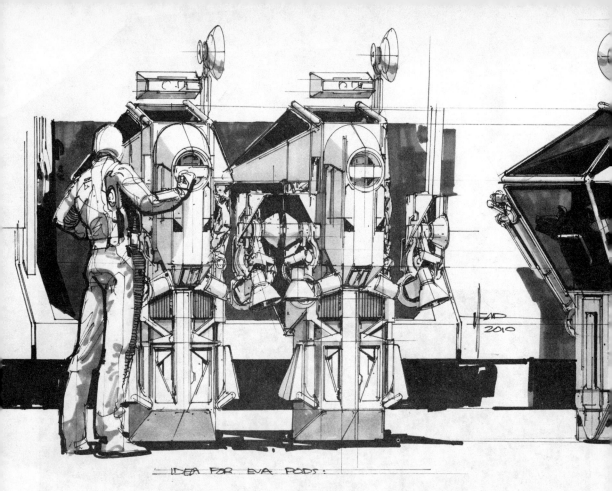

IDEA FOR EVA PODS:

This was the evolution of the manned pod.

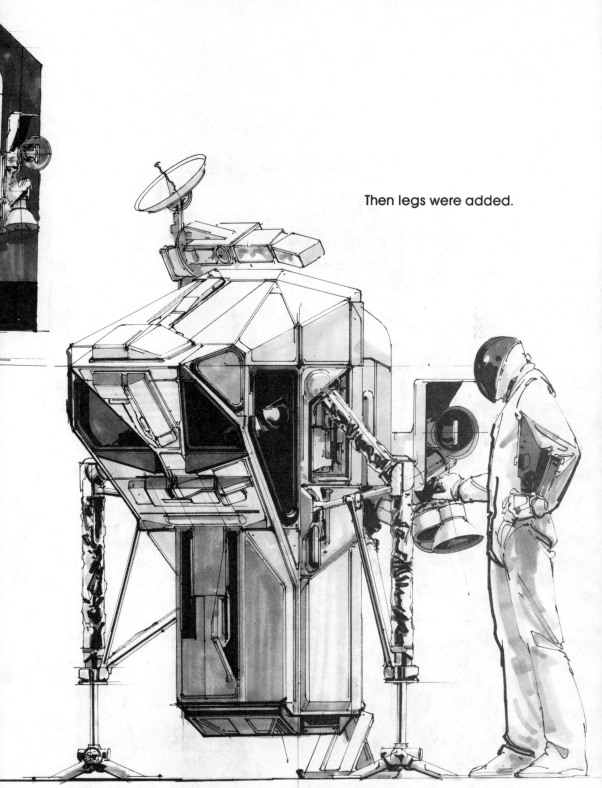

Then legs were added.

ONE MAN EVA POD FRONT 3/4.

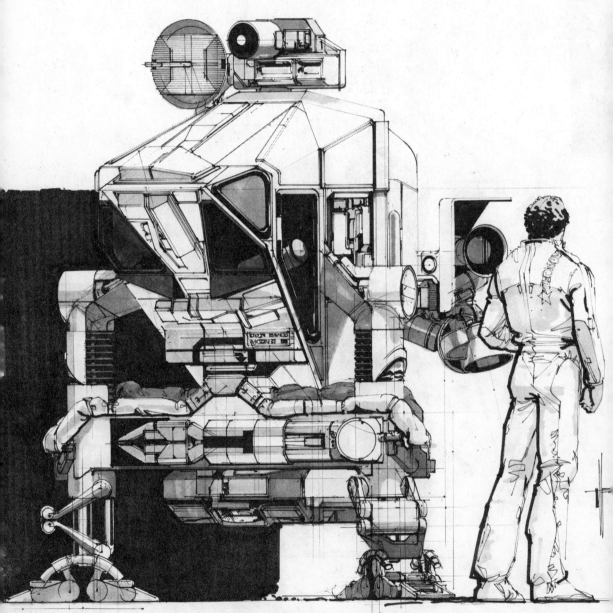

ONE MAN EVA POD: REVISION (LEGS) I

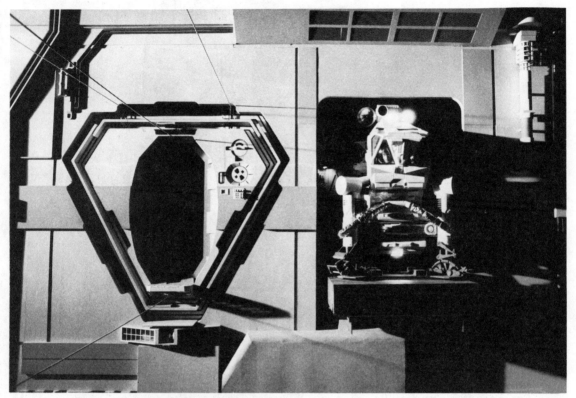

Max prepares to leave the *Leonov*.

With legs, it is complete. This is the unit used to investigate the surface of the monolith.

In the novel, Clarke describes a more tunnel-like structure. For more thrills and chills, Hyams came up with the idea of an "African rope bridge in space."

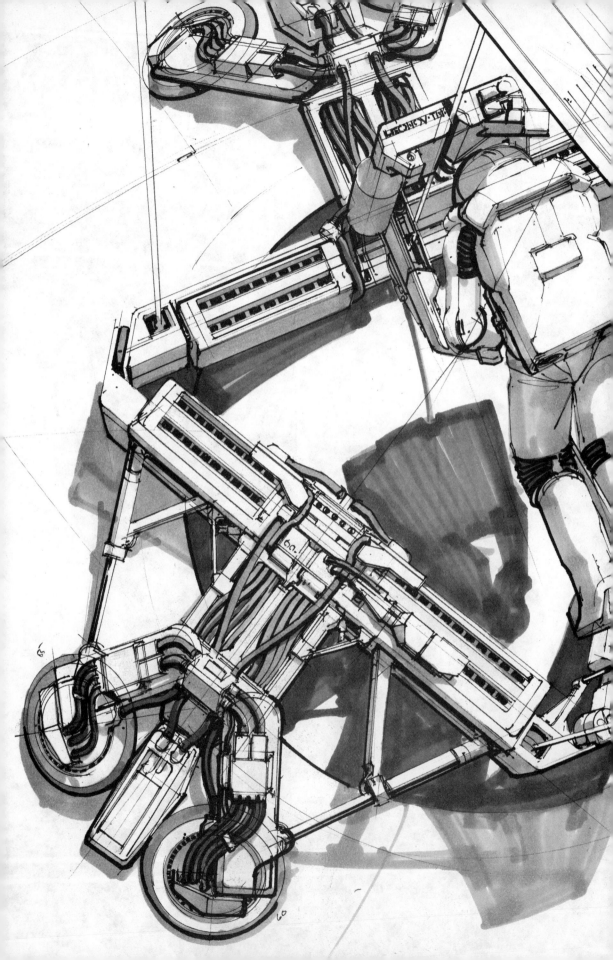

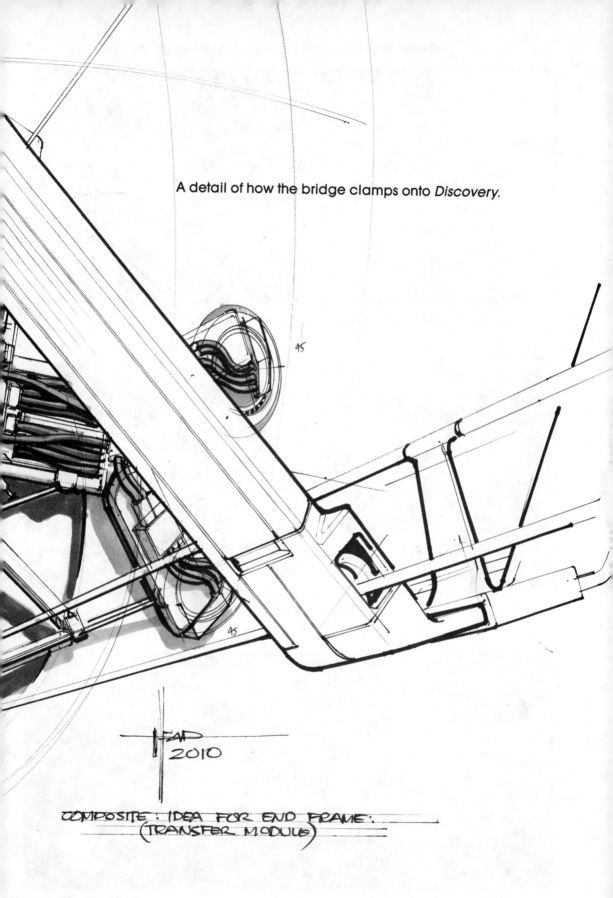

A detail of how the bridge clamps onto *Discovery*.

HEAD
2010

COMPOSITE: IDEA FOR END FRAME.
(TRANSFER MODULE)

These storyboards illustrate the use of the bridge.

INT. *Leonov* airlock: Latch whips open to reveal completed construction.

Chandra through frame.

Chandra makes his way to *Discovery*.

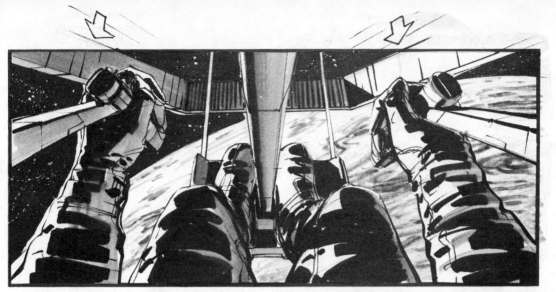

Chandra's POV looking down: Triangles flash by beneath T-bar.

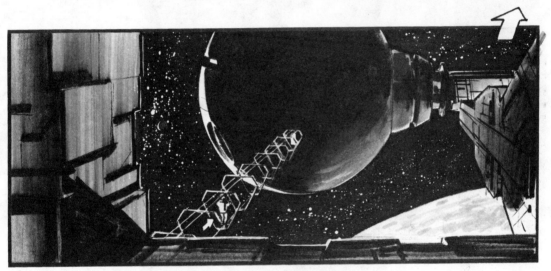

Tiny figure riding T-bar to *Discovery*.

The monolith hovers with T-bar in place.

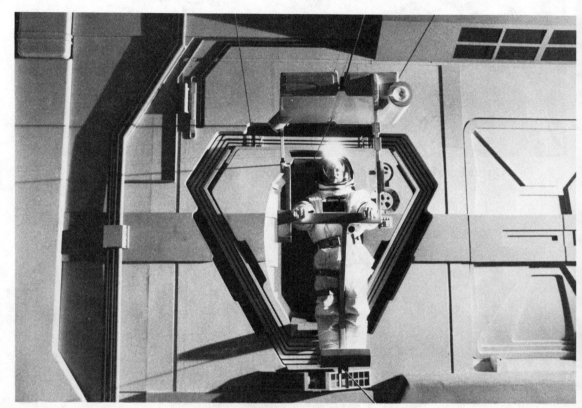

Chandra (Balaban) uses the tow bar.

CHAPTER II
THE *DISCOVERY*

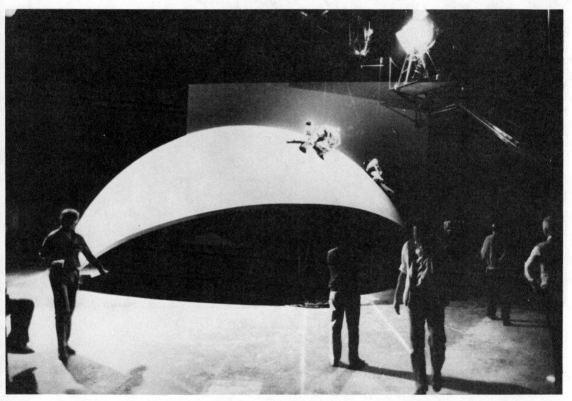

No plans, sketches, or models were left from *2001,* so all the *Discovery* set pieces had to be made from scratch. Using blow-ups from frames of the film, the production design team built what was required for *2010.* For the exterior shots, part of the ball and stem was all that was needed. These two set pieces were integrated with model work for all the *Discovery* sequences.

Peter Hyams checks lighting on the set of *Discovery*.

Discovery model in use.

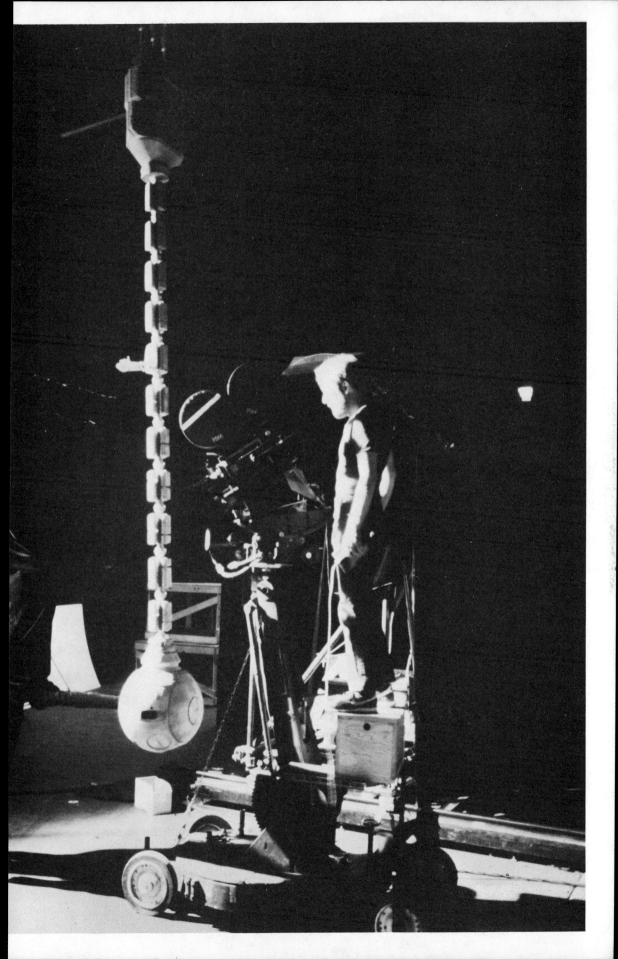

The *Leonov* and *Discovery* prepare to dock.

The bridge of *Discovery*.

The famous "brain" of HAL 9000.

This corridor leads to the pod bay of *Discovery*.

The pod bay.

CHAPTER III
THE STORY

For all the complicated action sequences that required both model/optical and live shots to work together, detailed storyboards were created so that everyone would know precisely what was needed.

Brailovsky and Curnow exit the *Leonov*.

They move away from the *Leonov*...

NEBULLA

ERUP

. . . as they move toward *Discovery*.

Its nose wipes frame . . .

. . . and reveals *Leonov*/two men.

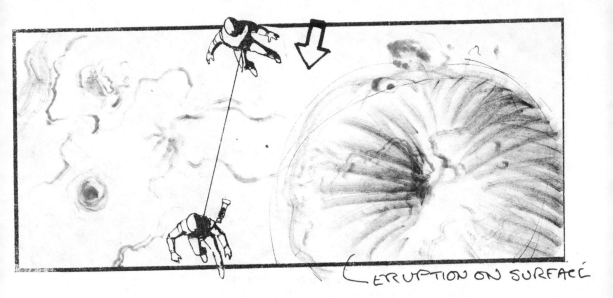

ERUPTION ON SURFACE

They move through shot as Io erupts, menacingly close.

ERUPTION ON HORIZON OF IO

As they move nearer to *Discovery* . . .

. . . its spinning becomes more ominous.

MOVING TO SHIP   NOT MOVING

About to grab on . . .

. . . Curnow is first to take hold.

SUN LIGHT

Brailovsky gets close as Curnow starts to spin.

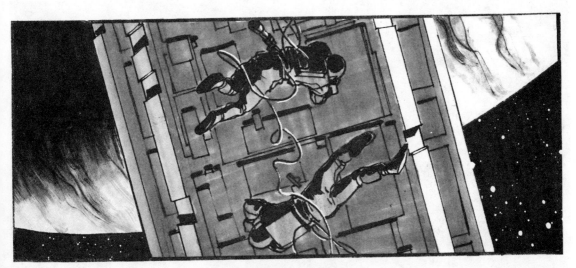

Brailovsky is next.

Curnow (Lithgow) grabs on to *Discovery*.

Curnow and Brailovsky approach *Discovery*.

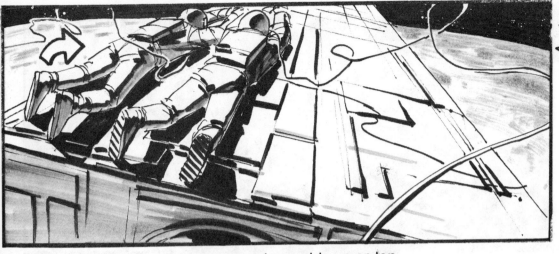

Then they crawl over side up on top.

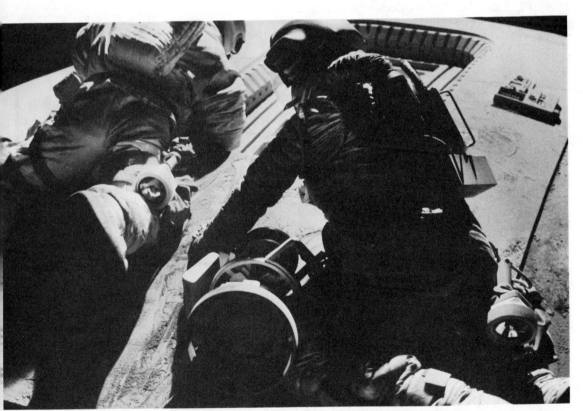

Curnow and Brailovsky reach the hatch of *Discovery*.

ERUPTION

Curnow and Brailovsky reach ball as *Discovery* continues to spin.

BG. 10 TRAVELS DOWN

They make their way over nose of *Discovery*.

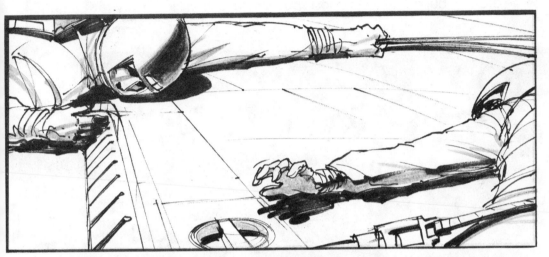

And Curnow reaches for latch.

Miniature dolls on a center landing point.

TINY
SPACEMEN
APPROACHING
DISC.

CHAPTER IV
CONSTRUCTION

From Syd Mead's intricate sketches grew even more intricate blueprints. Hyams was determined to faithfully duplicate these sketches. For six months, every man in Hollywood with a hammer was employed at MGM in order to build one of the most spectacular sets in film history.

Stage 30 on the MGM lot. In the foreground is the piece of the *Discovery* ball. The metal structure is a rotating "gimbel," enabling the set of the *Leonov* bridge to rotate. The tall wooden structure to the right is the HAL brain set.

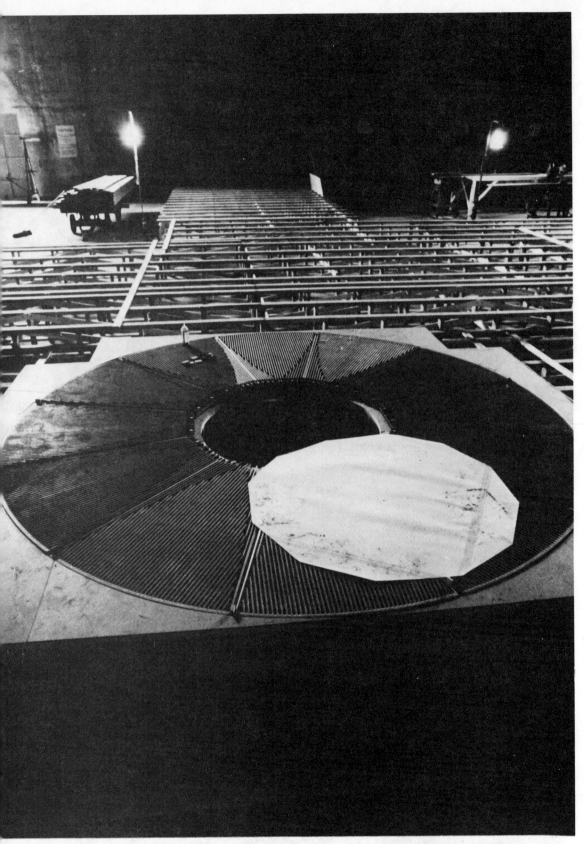

This is a view of the ward room looking toward the front of the ship. The round hole is where the ward room table will go.

The *Leonov* begins to take shape. This is a view similar to the prior ward room still.

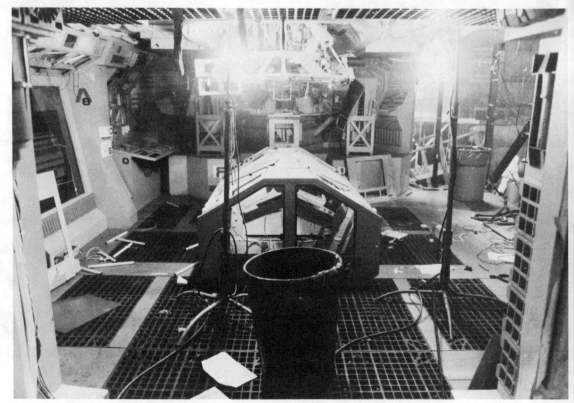

The bridge. In the foreground is the navigation console.

CHAPTER V
EARTH

In the novel *2010: Odyssey Two,* Arthur C. Clarke wrote about a wonderfully romantic house that Floyd and his marine-biologist wife lived in. This house was created and built over the old Esther Williams swim tank on the MGM lot. The tank had to be refurbished so that the dolphins would not hurt themselves on any protruding objects that the set was built on. For days, the trainers taught the dolphins the action Hyams desired. The shot was designed so that the audience would think they were in the ocean watching a dolphin. The shot follows the dolphin until it rises out of the water into someone's living room, where a child waits to feed him.

In keeping with the theme of the film—that of contact—the dolphins, who are so close to man in intelligence, worked perfectly in terms of achieving that thematic goal. They also provided a never-been-seen-before sequence.

Marineland trainer Tim Desmond runs through a practice session for director Peter Hyams and associate producer Jonathan A. Zimbert.

This is the scene all the practice was for.

This photo demonstrates how the shot was done. The crane dunks the camera and rises with the dolphins as they enter the living room.

Floyd prepares for the flight in his house as the two dolphins make a play for attention.

At the V.L.A. (Very Large Array) in Soccoro, New Mexico, the opening of the movie was filmed. Located in the middle of nowhere, scientists listen to the universe, hoping to make contact.

Peter Hyams sets up a shot along the long row of dishes at the V.L.A.